Spotlight on
Indonesia

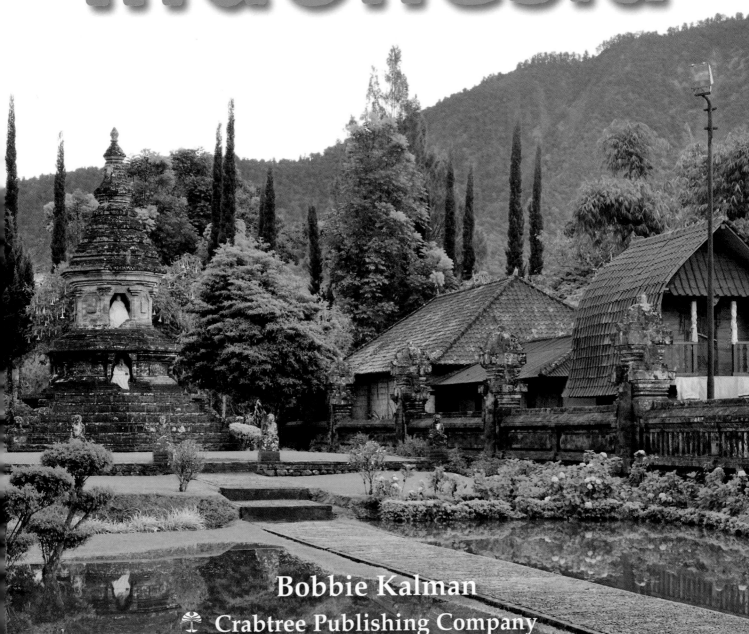

Bobbie Kalman

🌳 Crabtree Publishing Company

www.crabtreebooks.com

Spotlight On My Country

Created by Bobbie Kalman

For beautiful Kathy Berti,
who adds joy to my work every day

**Author and
Editor-in-Chief**
Bobbie Kalman

Editor
Kathy Middleton

Proofreader
Crystal Sikkens

Fact editor
Marcella Haanstra

Design
Bobbie Kalman
Katherine Berti

Photo research
Bobbie Kalman

Print and production coordinator
Katherine Berti

Prepress technician
Katherine Berti

Illustrations
Katherine Berti: page 5 (top map)

Photographs
Creatas: page 13 (tiger)
Photos.com: pages 18, 19 (top), 26 (top left)
Wikipedia: artist Nicolaas Pieneman:
     page 21 (top left)
Cover and all other images by Shutterstock

Library and Archives Canada Cataloguing in Publication

Kalman, Bobbie, 1947-
     Spotlight on Indonesia / Bobbie Kalman.

(Spotlight on my country)
Includes index.
Issued also in an electronic format.
ISBN 978-0-7787-3458-1 (bound).--ISBN 978-0-7787-3484-0 (pbk.)

     1. Indonesia--Juvenile literature. I. Title. II. Series: Spotlight
on my country

DS615.K34 2011   j959.8   C2010-904124-0

Library of Congress Cataloging-in-Publication Data

Kalman, Bobbie.
     Spotlight on Indonesia / Bobbie Kalman.
          p. cm. -- (Spotlight on my country)
     Includes index.
     ISBN 978-0-7787-3484-0 (pbk. : alk. paper) -- ISBN 978-0-7787-3458-1
(reinforced library binding : alk. paper) -- ISBN 978-1-4271-9537-1
(electronic (pdf))
     1. Indonesia--Juvenile literature. I. Title. II. Series.

DS615.K27 2011
959.8--dc22

                                        2010024604

Crabtree Publishing Company

www.crabtreebooks.com   1-800-387-7650
Printed in the U.S.A./082010/BA20100709

Published in Canada
Crabtree Publishing
616 Welland Ave.
St. Catharines, Ontario
L2M 5V6

Published in the United States
Crabtree Publishing
PMB 59051
350 Fifth Avenue, 59th Floor
New York, New York 10118

Published in the United Kingdom
Crabtree Publishing
Maritime House
Basin Road North, Hove
BN41 1WR

Published in Australia
Crabtree Publishing
386 Mt. Alexander Rd.
Ascot Vale (Melbourne)
VIC 3032

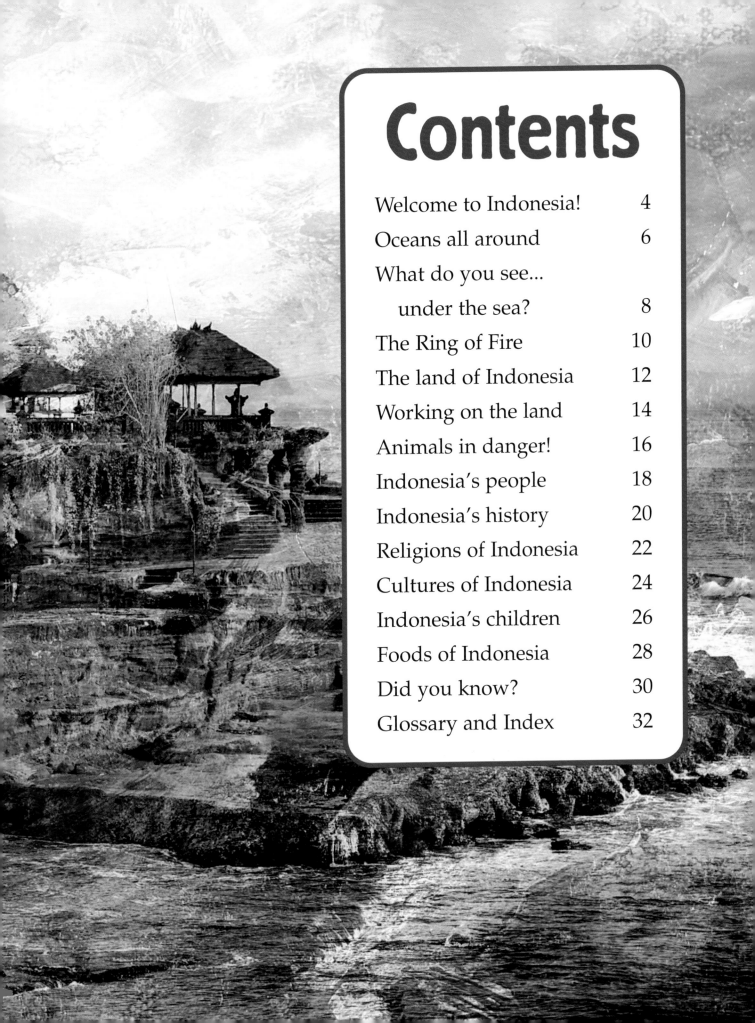

Contents

Welcome to Indonesia!

Indonesia is a **country** that is made up of 17,508 **islands**. A country is an area of land with **borders**, and an island is land that has water all around it. Indonesia is located mainly in the **continent** of Asia, but part of Indonesia is also in the continent of Australia/Oceania. A continent is a huge area of land. The other continents are North America, South America, Europe, Africa, and Antarctica. The seven continents are shown on the map on page 5. Indonesia is located at the **equator**. The equator is an imaginary line around the middle of Earth that divides Earth into two equal parts.

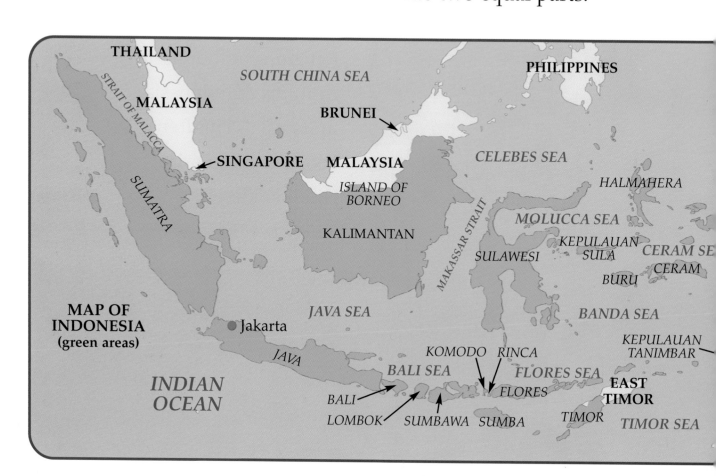

4

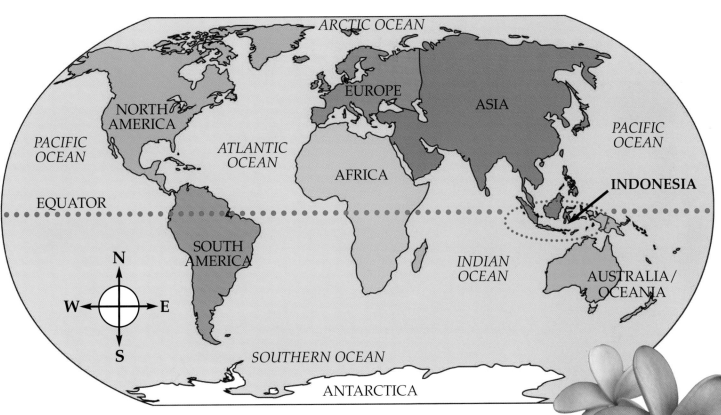

ARCTIC OCEAN

EUROPE

ASIA

NORTH
AMERICA

PACIFIC
OCEAN

PACIFIC
OCEAN

ATLANTIC
OCEAN

AFRICA

INDONESIA

EQUATOR

N

SOUTH
AMERICA

INDIAN
OCEAN

W E

AUSTRALIA/
OCEANIA

S

SOUTHERN OCEAN

ANTARCTICA

PACIFIC
OCEAN

EST
PUA

ISLAND OF
NEW GUINEA

PAPUA

**PAPUA
NEW
GUINEA**

KEPULAUAN
ARU

ARAFURA SEA

AUSTRALIA

Indonesia's neighbors

People live on 6,000 of Indonesia's islands. The five largest islands are Sumatra, Borneo (Kalimantan), New Guinea (Papua), Sulawesi, and Java. Indonesia's capital city, Jakarta, is on Java. Indonesia shares land borders with Malaysia, Papua New Guinea, and East Timor. Some of its islands also lie across seas and **straits**. A sea is a body of salt water that has land around it. The Flores Sea, Java Sea, and Celebes Sea are some examples. A strait is a narrow passage of water between land areas, which connects two seas or oceans.

5

Oceans all around

The thousands of islands of Indonesia form an **archipelago**. An archipelago is a chain of islands in a body of water, such as an ocean. The Indonesian Archipelago lies between the Indian Ocean and the Pacific Ocean. Seas and straits connect the two oceans. Warm water from the Pacific Ocean flows through the seas and straits to the Indian Ocean. Find the oceans, seas, and straits on the map at the bottom of pages 4 and 5.

Close to the islands are beautiful *coral reefs*. Coral reefs are ocean habitats with many kinds of fish and other animals. Coral reefs are made up of groups of tiny animals called coral *polyps*.

This island is called Flores. From this island, you can see many smaller islands across the water. Flores is one of the islands where Komodo dragons live. Find out about Komodo dragons on page 16.

This beach is in Papua. Papua is on the Pacific Ocean and is part of the continent of Australia/Oceania. It is on the same island as Papua New Guinea, a country that is not part of Indonesia.

What do you see...

The Java Sea, Celebes Sea, and Banda Sea are some of the seas that flow around the islands of Indonesia. The animals you see on these pages can be found in the coral reefs of these seas and in the Indian and Pacific oceans. So, what will you see under the sea? You will see some very amazing and weird fish that you may never have seen before!

*The fish above is a scorpionfish. It can change color to hide itself. Scorpionfish wait for **prey** to swim by. They then suck the prey animals into their mouths.*

pygmy seahorse

under the sea?

The pygmy seahorse matches the color and shape of the coral it lives on. It matches so well that it is hard to see the seahorse at all! Can you spot it? Look at the picture at the bottom of page 8 to see how it looks.

lure

This weird fish is called a hairy striped frogfish. It is hard to see because it blends in with the coral in the sea. The fish has a large wormlike **lure**, or bait, on its head. People put worms on their fishing poles to catch fish, but this fish has built-in bait for fishing.

eyes

Ornate ghost pipefish are related to seahorses. They feed mostly on tiny shrimps, which they snap up as the shrimp swim by. The heads of these two fish are facing down. Look at their eyes!

The Ring of Fire

Did you know that there are **volcanoes** under oceans as well as on land? A volcano is an opening in Earth's **crust**, or outer layer, which allows hot **magma**, ash, and gases to escape from below the earth. More than half of Earth's **active** volcanoes are in the Pacific Ocean in an area called the "Ring of Fire." It is an area where large numbers of **earthquakes** and volcanic **eruptions** occur. Some countries located in this area include the United States, Canada, Mexico, Indonesia, and Japan. Indonesia has more active volcanoes than any other country in the world.

Mount Semeru and Mount Bromo are two active volcanoes on the island of Java. Volcanoes that are active have erupted recently or may erupt at any time. Mount Semeru has erupted many times.

Mount Semeru is the highest volcano on the island of Java.

Mount Bromo is an active volcano.

Krakatau

Krakatau is the name of an island. It is also the name of the island's volcano. Krakatau has erupted many times, but in 1883, it killed thousands of people and filled all of Earth's atmosphere with volcanic dust.

The Kawah Ijen volcano in East Java is an active volcano. People are using the gases that escape from the volcano to earn a living. Miners use pipes to turn the gases into hot liquid sulfur, which then dries into hard yellow sulfur. The sulfur is used to make rubber and bleach for sugar. It is also used to make **cosmetics**, *or makeup. Working near this gas is very dangerous to people's health.*

The land of Indonesia

Indonesia's land has mountains, **valleys**, forests, and many volcanoes. Indonesia is a **tropical** country. A tropical country is near the equator and has a hot **climate**. Climate is the usual weather in an area. There are two seasons in Indonesia—the dry season and the wet season. During the wet season, a lot of rain falls.

Jakarta is the capital and largest city in Indonesia and the twelfth largest city in the world. More than eight million people live there. Jakarta is the center of business in Indonesia. Indonesia's **economy** *is one of the fastest growing in the world. Economy is the way a country makes money.*

This mountain village is in Papua.
Papua contains some of the highest mountains in the world.

monkeys

tiger

Forests cover more than half of Indonesia. Many kinds of animals live in the rain forests of Indonesia, including monkeys, apes, and tigers. Find out about the dangers these animals face on pages 16-17.

Working on the land

Almost half the people in Indonesia work on the land. They work as farmers and live in villages. Rice, tea, palm fruits, coffee, and spices are some of the crops that are grown in Indonesia.

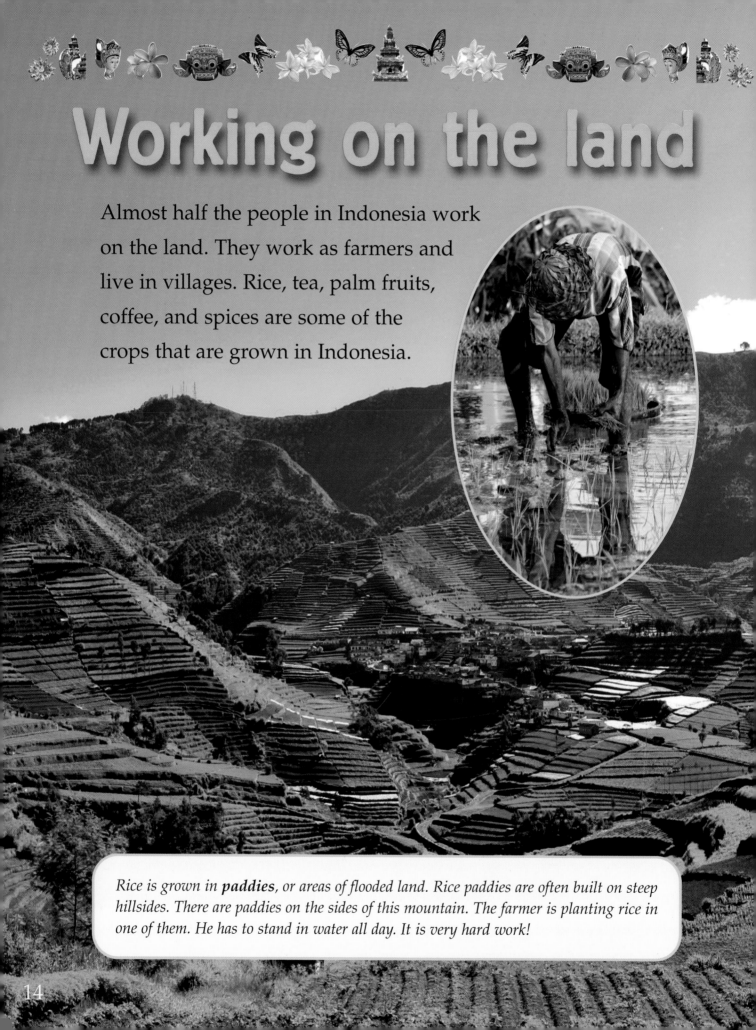

*Rice is grown in **paddies**, or areas of flooded land. Rice paddies are often built on steep hillsides. There are paddies on the sides of this mountain. The farmer is planting rice in one of them. He has to stand in water all day. It is very hard work!*

oil palm trees

palm oil seeds

Palm oil comes from the fruit of the oil palm tree. The oil is used in making different kinds of foods. It is also used as a clean-burning fuel for cars.

In the south of Kalimantan, there is a big floating market. Local farmers make trades with one another from their boats on the river. They sell mainly the fruits and vegetables that they have grown.

Animals in danger!

Some of the most magnificent animals on Earth live in Indonesia! Hundreds of thousands of different animal **species**, or types, live there. Unfortunately, Indonesia also has the greatest number of **endangered** species of animals. Endangered animals are in danger of dying out and disappearing from Earth forever. Animals such as parrots and orangutans are trapped and sold as pets in other countries. Many die before they reach their new homes. Find out which other Indonesian animals are endangered.

The palm cockatoo is a parrot that is sold as a pet.

Baby orangutans are very cute, so people also want them as pets.

The most famous Indonesian animal is the Komodo dragon. It is Earth's biggest lizard. Komodo dragons live on the islands of Flores, Rinca, and Komodo. They are losing their homes due to fires and earthquakes. Some cannot find food, and others are being hunted.

16

There are fewer than 60 Javan rhinoceroses left. These big animals were once hunted for their horns, which were used to make medicines. Today, people are trying to help these rhinos stay alive, but it is difficult. Javan rhino mothers have very few babies, so the number of rhinos is not growing. This rhino and its **calf**, or baby, live in a protected park.

The ebony langur is a monkey that lives in rain forests on the islands of Java, Bali, and Lombok. The langur is endangered because it is hunted for food. It is also losing its home because forests are being cut down to make room for farms.

There are between 400 and 500 Sumatran tigers left in the wild. Much of the rain forest where the tigers once lived has been cut down to grow oil palm trees. Indonesia has set aside parks to help save the tigers that are still alive, but many are being killed by **poachers**, or illegal hunters.

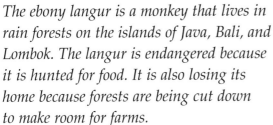

Indonesia's people

Indonesia has the fourth largest **population** on Earth, with over 242 million people. Population is the number of people who live in a country. Indonesia has more than 300 groups of people who have different **cultures**, or ways of life. Part of culture is food, clothing, music and dance, art, religion, and language. Indonesian is the main language of the country, but most people speak more than one language.

These children are Muslims, who follow a religion called Islam. They are wearing traditional Islamic clothing. Indonesia has the largest Muslim population in the world.

This girl lives on the island of Bali. The Balinese, or people of Bali, are known for their art, music, dance, and many festivals. Most Balinese follow the religion of Hinduism.

These children are Sasaks who live on Lombok Island. Long ago, the early Sasaks came to Lombok from Java.

This businesswoman lives in Jakarta. Jakarta is Indonesia's business center.

Indonesia's history

Most of the people who live in Indonesia came from Taiwan. Taiwan is a big island that is part of China. In the early days, people from India and China came to trade with Indonesia for rice and other foods. One of the most valuable plants that grew in Indonesia was the **nutmeg** plant, which brought European traders from Portugal, the Netherlands, and Great Britain to Indonesia.

nutmeg

cloves

Nutmegs and cloves were important spices. Both are used to make sweet treats.

Native Melanesian people lived in Indonesia before the people from Taiwan arrived. The **descendants** of the Melanesians now live mainly in Papua New Guinea and on some other islands, such as Fiji, Vanuatu, and the Solomon Islands, which are now part of an area called Melanesia.

The Dutch controlled Indonesia from 1800 to 1949.

Indonesia's first president was President Sukarno. He was the leader of the country until 1968.

*Since 2004, Indonesians have been able to **elect**, or choose, their own president and vice-president. These people are lining up to vote.*

Indonesia's name is the Republic of Indonesia. A republic is a country in which people vote for their leaders. Indonesia's flag is red and white.

Religions of Indonesia

Religion is a very important part of life in Indonesia. People practice a number of different religions in the country, but more than 85 percent of Indonesians are Muslim. Less than ten percent are Christian, and even fewer are Buddhist or Hindu. However, Hinduism is the main religion on the island of Bali. Hinduism was brought to Bali from India.

Tanah Lot means "Land in the Sea" in the Balinese language. Tanah Lot is a large rock in the ocean that is near the island of Bali. Long ago, a Hindu traveler named Nirartha spent the night on the little island and told the fishermen to build a temple on it where they could worship the sea gods. He felt that the rock was a holy place. Today, many people make long trips to visit this temple.

*The Muslim place of worship is called a **mosque**. This beautiful mosque is on the island of Sumatra.*

This young girl is reading the Qur'an, the holy book of Islam.

*Borobudur is a Buddhist monument in Java, Indonesia. The monument has 504 Buddha statues. The round structures are called **stupas**.*

Cultures of Indonesia

Much of Indonesia's culture is a mixture of Muslim, Hindu, and Buddhist religions. You can see the blend of cultures in food, music, dance, art, and theater. Some dances performed in Bali and Java, for example, act out stories about Buddhist and Hindu kings from long ago. Puppet theater, called Wayang, is performed by both Hindus and Muslims. The Muslim version, Wayang Kulit, uses puppets to create shadow figures.

There are many festivals in Bali. People in beautiful costumes parade through the streets, dance, and put on plays. These women are carrying offerings of food to the village temple.

24

These young dancers are performing a welcome dance at a "full-moon ceremony" in a village in Bali.

Wayang Golek puppet theater is performed in both Bali and Java.

Topeng is a kind of play in which dancers wear masks and perform stories about ancient heroes. Topeng dances are performed in Bali, Java, and on some other islands. "Topeng" means mask.

Indonesia's children

Most children in Indonesia live in villages. A village is a small community with a few houses. Indonesian children between six and twelve years of age attend primary school. Some schools are **public**, and some schools are **private** or religious. On many islands, children often wear Islamic clothing to school and modern clothing at home.

These boys attend elementary school. U.S. President Obama attended elementary school in Jakarta.

Some students take boats to school because their homes are in areas that are far away from their schools.

The children of Bali learn music, dance, and different kinds of art on their beautiful island.

Foods of Indonesia

Many kinds of fruits and vegetables grow in Indonesia all year long. The other foods that are plentiful are rice, fish, and seafood. Some of Indonesia's popular dishes contain these ingredients. The recipes for cooking foods were brought to Indonesia from India, China, and Europe. People in many countries today enjoy Indonesian dishes, such as **satay**. The spices of Indonesia, such as cloves and nutmeg, are used everywhere.

Food is a big part of religion and culture in Indonesia. These food baskets were carried to a Hindu temple in Bali on the heads of these women (see page 24). They contain the colorful fruits of Bali.

(above) These delicious desserts are made with fruits, cake, and chocolate. YUM!

(right) Satay is meat that is grilled on a stick. It tastes great with a salad but is often eaten with rice and peanut sauce.

Did you know?

There are many fascinating facts about Indonesia. Look at the pictures on these two pages and then take part in our Indonesian treasure hunt on page 31!

(below) Rafflesia flowers are the world's biggest flowers. Some are as big as 39 inches (100 cm) when measured across the center from one side to the other. Rafflesia plants have no stems, leaves, or roots. They smell like rotting meat.

(above) The tarsier is one of the world's smallest **primates**. *A primate is a very smart mammal. Monkeys, apes, lemurs, and people are primates. The eastern tarsier can be found on the island of Sulawesi and on some nearby islands.*

*In 2004, a **tsunami** killed nearly 230,000 people. Tsunamis are enormous waves that hit land with great force. This tsunami was caused by a huge earthquake in the Indian Ocean. More than half a million people lost their homes in Indonesia. Homeless people had to live in tent cities like this one.*

Treasure hunt

Read the clues and find the "treasures" in the book.

1. Which spice "treasure" brought people from Europe to Indonesia?
2. What is the biggest lizard on Earth?
3. Name an island on which it lives.
4. What is a Muslim house of worship called?
5. What is the "ring" of volcanoes called?
6. In which ocean is it?
7. What food is grilled on a stick?
8. What are the colors of the Indonesian flag?
9. Which American president attended elementary school in Indonesia?
10. Which big endangered cat lives on the island of Sumatra?

Answers

1. nutmeg 2. Komodo dragon
3. Flores, Komodo, or Rinca
4. mosque 5. Ring of Fire
6. Pacific Ocean 7. satay
8. red and white 9. President
Obama 10. Sumatran tiger

Glossary

Note: Some boldfaced words are defined where they appear in the book.

border An imaginary line that separates countries or areas of land

coral reef An area of the ocean that is made up of live coral polyps and dead corals

cosmetics Makeup that is put on the face, hair, or other parts of the body

descendant Someone who is related to a person who lived many years before

earthquake A violent shaking of the ground

endangered Describing an animal or plant species that is in danger of dying out

eruption An explosion of lava, gases, ash, and rocks through a volcano

magma Liquid rock found deep inside Earth

poacher A person who hunts and kills animals illegally, or against the law

polyp A tiny ocean animal with a soft round body and tentacles around its mouth

population The total number of people who live in a certain place

prey An animal that is hunted by another animal for food

private school A school that is not run by the government and charges money from its students

public school A school run by the government, which students attend for free

species A group of closely related living things that can make babies together

tropical Describing areas with hot climates found near the equator

tsunami An giant wave created by an earthquake or volcanic eruption underwater

valley An area of low land between hills

Index